Good luck, de bewti!

Keith Skipper Tony Hall

GW00630956

RUSTIC REVELS

A BEWTIFUL CROP OF COUNTRY LARFS!

KEITH SKIPPER
tells the yarns

TONY HALL
draws the pictures

NOSTALGIA
Publications
brings them together

Arggh!

Published by:
NOSTALGIA PUBLICATIONS
(Terry Davy)
7 Elm Park, Toftwood,
Dereham, Norfolk, NR19 1NB

First Impression 1997

© Nostalgia Publications 1997

ISBN 0 947630 17 1

All rights reserved. No part of this publication may
be reproduced, stored in a retrieval system, or
transmitted in any form or by any means, electronic,
mechanical, photocopying, recording, or otherwise,
without prior permission of the publisher.

Designed and Typesetting:
NOSTALGIA PUBLICATIONS

Printed by:
COLOURPRINT
Fakenham, Norfolk

Front cover photograph reproduced by courtesey of Brian Hedge

Contents

Acknowledgements

Mr. Skipper: I think we ought to thank a few people for help with this publication.

Mr. Hall: You do that. You're far more erudite and efficacious with words. I prefer to speak through my illustrations.

Mr. Skipper: What on earth do they say?

Mr. Hall: They provide the odd hint that this boy is a modest genius.

Mr. Skipper: We owe it to all our families and friends for their support and inspiration. Special thanks to our dear wives ...

Mr. Hall: Very dear round the shops!

Mr. Skipper: ... for laughing at the right times. Let us add genuine expressions of gratitude to publisher Terry Davy for bringing us together, to the Eastern Daily Press for featuring our humble talents so regularly and to those who have shared amusing yarns over the years.

Mr. Hall: Creep!

Mr. Skipper: But you have to admit I do it rather well.

Introduction

by Keith Skipper

This mission of mirth is fraught with danger.

Any collection of local yarns, polished and cherished though it might be, invites a number of serious allegations. Some are impossible to fight off effectively.

Many stories have done, or are still doing, the rounds elsewhere and have merely been given a local lick of paint.

Most of those colourfully coated in dialect were created to be told rather than read.

Several included in a volume like this were inspired by a closely-knit agricultural world long disappeared over the headlands.

Well, confession is good for the soul, and even the most parochial of countrymen will admit it is some time since horses and binders starred with up to 40 men in a Norfolk or Suffolk harvest field.

The farming revolution, accelerated since the last war by the rise of agri-business barons, has drastically reduced the size of the country cast directly involved with the land. It follows that a different stage attracts different actors and a new collection of stories.

Deep and durable affection for the past, especially in more remote rural corners, may keep the scythe and the seed-fiddle just ahead of the commuter and computer when it comes to ripping yarns in the village pub. But harsh realities all too often flatten bucolic images as country life moves into a faster, busier and noisier lane.

So, isn't this just a sigh of nostalgia on the wind of change? A well-meaning but ultimately futile gesture in the face of a technologically-driven march towards uniformity? A typically cussed pebble of native defiance dropped in the ocean of standardisation?

It may be all of them - but the mission is still worth undertaking. I have been coaxed on to a new launching-pad by much more than rampant nostalgia and a lingering delight in waging war against insuperable odds.

I was weaned on country humour, some of it barbed and highly personalised, and I like to think it helped prepare me for the serious challenges to come ... work in the media, marriage, parenthood, losing my hair, failing a string of driving tests and trying to convince anyone prepared to listen that the minority is always wrong - at the beginning.

One of a family of ten brought up in a small cottage in the middle of agricultural Norfolk, I recall the decade after the last war dominated by babies, nappies, tin baths and the copper boiling furiously up the kitchen corner. Feeding the fire with wood was one of my regular jobs.

We thrived on big-family jokes I hear recycled today by folk raised in a home with electricity, a bathroom and indoor toilets. They were luxuries in our 1950s book when laughter lines were lit by hissing Tilley lamp and leaping flames from freshly-sawn logs:-

"That kettle's boiled - better send for the midwife!"

"There are so many nappies drying in here I can see a rainbow in the front room!"

"Just knock a hole in the wall so we can dip our bread in next door's gravy!"

"Mum can't afford Andrew's Liver Salts, so she's going to sit us on the potty and tell ghost stories!"

"Mrs Jones has got a Norfolk spin dryer - a hula-hoop with pegs on it!"

"Do you think they will buy me a hat so I can look out of the window?"

Little social comments in their way on country life some 40 years ago when a bath in front of the fire was commonplace and a visit to the little house at the bottom of the garden an expedition full of menace after dark. Being led down the garden path by an older sister or brother had its attractions.

Many of the yarns I have included in this book come from that era of rural austerity, an era with which my artistic colleague Tony Hall can also identify with a twinkle in his eye. The fact we could tune in to a similar wavelength has made it even more fun to amble along together in the cause of local culture. The fact we cannot muster a decent head of hair between us will be cited by some as a more pertinent pointer to a sympathetic partnership.

We could have featured the sweet old chestnut about the balding middle-aged man who asked his barber: "Why do you charge me the full price for cutting my hair - there's so little of it?"

"Well," said the barber, "actually I make very little charge for cutting it. What you are really paying for is my searching for it!"

Perhaps we'll save that one for another twin project. In the meantime, savour these rustic yarns and illustrations, treating familiarity as one of the strengths of a fast-changing area where humour has an important part to play in breaking down barriers.

And always think twice before you laugh at a country tale. The laugh might be on you.

Keith Skipper

Cromer, 1997

Chapter One

Out of the Mouths...

Children should be careful what they say. Parents are always repeating what they hear

It used to be fashionable - and some would say desirable - for children to be seen and not heard. "Speak when you are spoken to, and not until!" was a common instruction accompanied by a warning finger, especially when Sunday tea-time company was expected. The good name of the family had to be preserved.

That out of such a climate of restraint at home and school, and in the local community as a whole, should come such a rich fund of country yarns speaks volumes for youthful invention and resilience. And an acceptance that a clip round the ear could well be worth it on certain occasions.

There are countless examples from the village classroom where a less-than-average pupil confronted by a gloating teacher and smug colleagues has pulled out a sizzling iron from the fire:-

Teacher: "So, 'excavate' means 'to hollow out'. Billy, you're a genius with words. Just give me a sentence including the word 'excavate'."

Billy: (after a long silence punctuated by giggles all around him) "I dropped a heavy sack o'tearters on my Dad's toe - an' he excavated!"

Children broke down barriers with humour, even if some of it was scarcely intended. They broke rules with witty and clever answers, even if those responses simply camouflaged or confirmed ignorance. They emerged from the shadows to take stern and overbearing grown-ups down a peg or two, even if it did lead to swift retribution.

There are fewer restrictions nowadays on youngsters' behaviour. Computers have pushed aside cowboys. Street credibility takes over too soon from playground adventure. The passing of a world harbouring more obvious order and lingering innocence is mourned by another generation ... and then celebrated in a selection of favourite yarns where young voices disarm, deflate and delight.

Baby Care

It was time for the nativity play in a Norfolk village school. Mary and Joseph greeted the arrival of Baby Jesus, folded him carefully in teacher's shawl and placed him lovingly in the plant pot trough serving as a crib.

Joseph asked if the boy was behaving himself. That was the cue for Mary to show her ad-libbing skill.

"Well, he ent ser bad darin' the day. But he's a little sod at nights!"

... he's a little sod at nights!

Tork Proper

The village schoolmistress was working overtime to teach the class good grammar.

"One should never say 'I saw him do it'" she said.

"Yis" piped up Charlie at the back, "speshully if yew ent sure he dunnit!"

A Class Reply

Many years ago an inspector paid a call at a Norfolk village school. Those were the days when the headmaster got paid according to how much he had taught his pupils - and they didn't want to let him down.

Well, the inspector came into the classroom and said to the headteacher "I'll just give your class a little test on numbers." He took a bit of chalk, went to the blackboard and said "Would some boy or girl give me a number, please, and I'll write it down."

Billy Jones shouted out "Sixty-three, Sir". He turned round and wrote on the board thirty-six. He turned back and looked at the class. Nobody spoke or flickered an eyelid.

The inspector turned to the headteacher and said "I'll try again. Can someone else give me a number?"

Mary Parker, sitting in the back row, stood up and said "Fifty-nine, Sir." He turned round and wrote ninety-five on the board. Again he looked at the class. Again nobody moved or spoke. With a sigh of exasperation he whispered to the headteacher "You've got a pretty poor lot here, but I'll give them one more chance. Right, can anyone else give me a number?"

Little Sammy Starling, sitting in the front row, jumped up and shouted "Thatty-three, Marster - an' dew yew beggar that one about!"

Load of Bull

The village parson was surprised to meet one of his smallest Sunday School pupils driving a large cow along a narrow lane.

"Good morning, Lucy. Where are you going with that splendid beast?"

"Please, sar, I'm a' tearkin' ole Buttercup ter be bulled."

"Goodness me, but couldn't your father do that?"

"Oh no, sar ... that hev ter be a bull!"

In the Wings

Some village youngsters were playing Mums and Dads in the lane as the parson came by. He smiled, and then saw one small disconsolate child sitting round the corner well away from the rest. He asked why he wasn't playing with the others.

"But I am, sar" said the little one.

"And what part are you playing, then?"

"Please sar, I'm a little ole bearby woss waitin' ter be born!"

Food for Thought

The vicar had been invited to lunch. The two small sons of the household were upset because, in order to feed him in the expected manner, two of the backyard roosters had been killed for the occasion.

They sat silently through the meal while the vicar tucked in. As the family dutifully saw him off, the last of the roosters perched on the garden wall gave a loud "Cock-a-doodle-doo!".

"My word!" said the vicar, "What a proud bird he is!"

One of the little lads could contain himself no longer. "And so he orter be, raverend" he sobbed. "He hev got tew sons in the ministry!"

Can't Miss Him

Jimmy answered the knock on the farmhouse door to find a stranger standing there.

"Is your father in?" he asked.

"No, bor, that he ent" said Jimmy. "He's down a 'muckin the pigs out. Dew yew go down that there loke past the barn. Yew'll find him down there ...

"He'll be the one wi' the hat on!"

Waste Not ...

A young lad turned up at the village shop just before closing time on Saturday evening.

"Toylet roll, please mister."

The kindly old shopkeeper took one down from the shelf and handed it over.

First thing Monday morning the boy was there as the door was being unlocked. He had the toilet roll under his arm. He strode to the counter and thrust the roll towards the shopkeeper ...

"Mum say kin yew tearke it back - cumpany dint cum!"

Taking a Stand

The village teacher said to Charlie's class, "Will all those who think they might be stupid please stand up."

For a moment no one stirred. Then Charlie got to his feet.

"Charles" said the teacher, "Do you think you are stupid?"

"No, nut really, Miss," he replied. " I just dint like ter see yew standin' there by yarself!"

Fruity Reply

Young Walter was caught red-handed scrumping apples in Farmer Parker's orchard.

"Didn't you see my notice?" asked the irate farmer.

"Cors I did" replied Walter, "But that said 'Private', so I dint read enny more!"

Happy Corner

The parson was talking to the youngest children at Sunday School. He asked Ben: "Do you know where little boys and girls go when they do bad things?"

"Cors I dew" said Ben ... "behind Farmer Smith's barn!"

Tasty Morsel

The bell rang for the end of playtime and the children raced back into school. The next lesson was arithmetic. A rather backward pupil was singled out to answer questions about fractions, much to the obvious delight of his colleagues.

"Now, boy" said the teacher, "which would you prefer - a third of a cake or a fifth of a cake?"

The boy replied without hesitation: "Fifth of a cearke, sar!"

The teacher was very cross and demanded to know the reason for such an answer. The reply was again rapidly forthcoming:

"Please, sar, ter tell yew the truth, I ent tew keen on cearke!"

Last Rites

The tearful children were holding a funeral service in the back garden for their recently-demised hamster. As they lowered him into his final resting place, a small boy closed his eyes and said solemnly "In the nearme o' the Father, the Son - and in the hole he goest. Armin."

Final Word

Young Bertie's father had recently died and the village rector was having a friendly chat with the lad.

"Now, what were dear Father's last words?" he inquired.

"Dunt think he hed none" said Bertie, "Mum wuz wi' him right up tew the end!"

Mum wuz wi' him right up tew the end!

Chapter Two

Close to Nature

God made the country, and man made the town

The most ardent advocates of country life would be reluctant to claim all answers rest in the soil. But too many rural stories carry an earthy edge to deny the deep-rooted influence of nature in the raw.

An amiable bluntness pervades the majority of farmyard tales. There's no shyness in accepting the roles of bull, boar and cockerel. Newcomers to the country may be embarrassed by this no-nonsense approach to sex education - but that's half the fun.

Nor are colourful graduates of the Agricultural Academy of Squit slow to score points off each other, although exercises have been cut in recent years by falling numbers on the land. A worker can spend days on end cocooned in a tractor cab, covering hundreds of acres without seeing or talking to anyone else.

There's more dust and noise than banter and camaraderie about the corn harvest picture these days. The coronation of the year has been shorn of much of its majesty by the march of mechanisation, but there remain loyal subjects along the headlands to keep the old country wit and repartee alive, even if that means sending unsuspecting boys to the local shop for a tin of striped paint or a packet of hurdle seed.

They say that to live in the country you need the soul of a poet, the mind of a philosopher, the simple tastes of a hermit and a good four-wheel drive vehicle. Add to that an obligatory sense of humour.

Newcomer: *"Excuse me, but could you use me on the land?"*

Farmer: *"Sorry - we have special stuff for that nowadays!"*

Sole Companions

Fred and Ernie were stretched out opposite each other on the barn floor eating their grub.
"Thass time yew hed them boots mended, bor" said Fred. "I should think they let the water in dunt they?"
"Yis they dew" said Ernie, "But they let it out agin!"

Yis they dew . . . but they let it out agin!

Spreading the Load

An old man and a young lad were muck-spreading on the farm. The master watched them from the gate. He walked up and said to the lad: "George I've been watching you two at work and I could not help but notice that your elder colleague is spreading two forkfuls to your one."

"Yis, Marster, I know" said George. "I keep a'tellin' the silly ole fewl, but he tearke no notice o' me!"

The Right Price

A farmer, his wife and eldest son George went away for a holiday after harvest. They left Billy in charge. He was none too bright - some said a couple of sandwiches short of a picnic.

The following day a neighbouring farmer paid a call, accompanied by his daughter; "Can I speak to your parents?"

"No, they hev gone away for the weekind."

"Can I speak to George, then?"

"No, he he' gone with 'em ... they left me in charge. Kin I help?"

"Well, your brother, George, has made my daughter pregnant, and I want to know what you are going to do about it." Billy scratched his head, looked very serious and thought for a minute.

"I carnt rightly help yer ... I know how much Farther charge fer the ole bull - but I dunt know how much he charge fer George."

Good Remedy

Percy went in for pig-keeping. He had four sows and a boar. Come the Spring and the old boar wouldn't do his job. Percy rang the vet and he sent some tablets round. They did the job. The boar performed splendidly.

Come next Spring, and the boar was again in a reluctant mood. Percy rang the vet.

"Now last year yew sent me some tablets ... kin I hev a few more?"

"Well, how big were they?"

"Oh, I carnt remember."

"What colour were they then?"

"I carnt remember - but they tearste a bit like aniseed."

Matter of Trust

Ephraim and Bert were working together in the field and had been sitting under the hedge enjoying their dinner. When they got up to start work again, Ephraim felt in his pocket for something and discovered he had lost a shilling. They started looking for it.

After a while something Ephraim said made Bert exclaim; "Here, yew ent insiniratin' I're got yar shillin', are yew Ephraim?"

"Oh no, but I're got a feelin' somehow if yew hent bin helpin' ter look forrit, I myter found it!"

Cautious Man

Old Charlie was receiving nine shillings a week for working on the farm. The master approached him one morning and said: "Reckon you deserve a rise, Charlie. You can draw another shilling a week."

"Thankyer Marster. I'll think it over."

Next day Charlie met his master and said: "If thass all the same ter yew, I dunt think I'll tearke that rise."

"But why ever not Charlie? You put in a lot of hours here."

"Well, Marster, thass like this here ... if I miss harf a day, look how much more munny I'll hev ter lose!"

Job for Ben

It had been a good harvest and the farmer was in a jovial mood. He thought he would have a bit of fun with old Ben who was supposed to be a few sticks short of a bundle.

"Now, Ben I want you to take a wheelbarrow and a four-tined fork and empty all the water out of the horsepond so it can be replenished when we get a good rain."

Old Ben wandered off and collected the fork and barrow. The farmer stood smirking as he passed. Suddenly Old Ben turned ... "Now, Marster, afore I git on a'dewin' the pond, what dew yew want me ter dew wi' the water - spreed it or leave it in piles!"

Brave Offer

A man strode up to a farmhouse and tapped on the door. When the farmer answered the man said; "I really am very sorry, but I've just run over your cockerel. However, you'll be pleased to hear that I would like to replace it."

The farmer smiled benevolently. "Well, I dunt know how yew'll mearke out, but the hins are round the back!"

Steps to Recovery

Arthur accidentally lost his lunchbox down a well while he and Amos were working. They looked down and saw it floating on the water. They let the bucket down and tried to swing it in the hope of getting the box in - but to no avail.

"What we want is a ladder" said Amos. "I'll go an'see if I kin borrer one orf ole Hinry."

A short time later Amos returned empty-handed. "Wunt he let yew hev one?" asked Arthur.

"Well, he'd let me hev one" Amos told him. "Trubble wuz we want one ter go down; Hinry'd only got one yew go up on!"

The Last Straw

Ezra, Bill and Charlie were stacking straw bales in the barn when the bales collapsed, leaving Charlie underneath them. His companions quickly set to work hauling the bales away, but they found their mate unconscious. Ezra took charge.

"Yew sit him up an' loosin his collar while I tearke his pulse."

Holding Charlie's wrist in one hand and his old pocketwatch in the other Ezra looked quite worried. "Thass a rum'un. He's either a gonner or my watch hev stopped."

Sound Advice

Fred and Ernie were working on fields well away from the farm. One morning Fred turned up late. That afternoon about half an hour before leaving-off time, he started packing up his things.

"Hold yew hard!" said Ernie. "That ent knockin' orf time yit."

"I know" said Fred "but I wuz allus told that dunt dew ter be learte twice in one day!"

No Fowl Play

Horry kept chickens in the old barn which stood alongside the main road running through the village. The floor of the barn was considerably lower than the road. So when the water main burst the barn was flooded and the hens all drowned.

Horry put in a claim to the water authority for compensation. Some time later he called his neighbour to tell him a cheque had come for £25.

"Blarst, thass good. Yew'll be able ter buy sum more hins now."

"Nut bloomin' likely" said Horry "I'm gittin' ducks this time!"

Slow Learner

Tom won most prizes as usual at the village horticultural show. The vicar presented him with his prizes and asked how he always managed to do so well.

"Manewer" said Tom. "Good rotten manewer. All I ever use is manewer."

Tom went off proudly with his prizes. The vicar turned to Tom's wife. "He is a remarkable gardener - but I wonder if you could teach him to say fertiliser instead of manure."

She looked him straight in the collar. "Well, I'll do my best, Wikker, - but thass took nigh on ten year ter git him ter call it manewer!"

Chapter Three

Ancient Wisdom

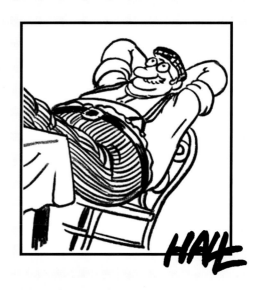

The worst thing about getting old is having to listen
to a lot of advice from your children

When the pace of life was slower and communities were smaller, closer and more inclined to listen to each other, village elders held a special place in rural affections.

Age and wisdom could go together without patronising nods and smiles or sneering references to rampant nostalgia. Those consulted gave off a contentment born of a narrow horizon, it's true, but though they may not have been far, they saw plenty.

Constancy, security and an acceptance of what fate had decreed were at the heart of these little parliaments sitting in the pub corner, by the boundary's edge or on a favourite seat in the shade. They preached old-fashioned virtues even when a fast-changing world was just around the corner.

Apart from the amount of local knowledge ready to be released with clouds of pipe tobacco smoke, not least for the benefit of occasional newcomers and tourists, there was often a twinkling sense of fun to turn a history lesson into memorable entertainment.

Jacob and Maria were elevated to the rustic peerage - "Mines of information ... and they put it across so well!" - and it was only natural that the stories should become ever-so-slightly embellished as requests poured in for another airing.

Television, telephones and a reluctance to walk even a few yards up the street have combined to make impromptu storytelling an endangered art. Ironically, demand for memories, preferably in a rich coating of local dialect, has never been stronger.

Technology can help meet that demand to some extent, but we ought to cherish more the genuine articles in all their natural glory.

A Real Tonic

Bert went to a Temperance lecture in the village hall. He enjoyed pictures of what the speaker called "sour roses" of the liver.

Then the lecturer put two glasses on the table and filled one with water and the other with whisky. He took a live worm and dropped it into the water. The worm wriggled and he said "Look how it is enjoying the pure water."

Then he put the worm into the whisky. It sank to the bottom, stone dead.

"Now, dear friends. You can see the evil effects of alcohol. Would any member of the audience like to ask a question?"

"'Scuse me, Marster," said Bert, "but could yew tell me the brand of that there whisky?"

"I can't see how that has anything to do with the matter, but if you really want to know it is Johnny Walker."

"Thankyer werry much" said Bert. "I he' suffered from worms fer years!"

29

Still Intact

After an earth tremor in 1931, a Norfolk labourer was asked by a local newspaper reporter if he had felt it.

"Blarst, no, I dint ... I sleep at the back o' the house."

Then there was an old lady telling of her experiences:

"That wuz suffin terrible, that wuz ... th' ole house begin ter rock an' shearke, and th'ole bed along wi'it. My ole man, he get up and look outer the winder and I haller out 'John!' I say, ' I berleeve thass the ind o' the wald woss cum!' 'Yis, Maria' he say, ' I berleeve that hev ... no! thass orryte, them shallots is still there!'"

True Colours

On reaching the age of 70 a Suffolk maiden aunt turned her thoughts to the inevitable. She decided to make arrangements for her funeral. "I hent never bin berholden ter ennywun in my life, an' I ent gorter start now." she mused.

Off she went to see the village undertaker. She was invited to select lining material for the coffin. The undertaker said: "We normally bury the married women with a deep purple lining, but unmarried women like yourself usually have a nice piece of white taffeta."

The old dear thought for a while. "I tell yew what," she said eventually. "Yew kin use the white taffeter, but kin yew trim th'edjes wi' papple jist ter let 'em know I had my moments!"

Be Prepared

There was a hosepipe ban on all gardens and the village looked very parched. All except old John's garden. The man from the water company was a bit suspicious and called round to warn old John not to use mains water for his flowers and vegetables.

"Dunt yew fret bor. When we're got plenty, we use it sparingly ... so when we hent got enny, we're allus got sum!"

Pass Master

A country chap was feeling under the weather and had to visit the doctor in a village three miles away. The doctor examined him.

"Now, have you passed anything this morning, Hector?"

"Oh, yis" said Hector, smiling, "tew loads o' straw, five bikes and a gret ole steamroller!"

... tew loads o' straw, five bikes and a gret ole steamroller!

Too Sudden

On hearing of the death of King George V, a Norfolk farmworker showed deep distress. Then he quietly remarked: "If yew'd a'told me afore, that wunt he'cum ser sudden."

Sartorial Tip

The old village parson had retired, and the new incumbent was biking round the parish to meet members of his flock.

As he passed the pub, The Eradicated Coypu, he called out cheerily "Good morning, gentlemen." to two local veterans sipping their pints outside.

"Thass our new parsun" said George. "He's a rum'un ... got seven kids an'nuther wun on the way."

"Oh, ah" said Charlie. "Oh, ah ... he wotter wear his trowsers searme way he wear his collar!"

Train of Thought

Billy and his wife were getting on an excursion train bound for Yarmouth at Ellingham station when they were told they would not have to change at Beccles as usual.

"They're going to hitch this train to the other one" explained the porter.

Sure enough, at Beccles the Waveney Valley carriages were shunted onto the rear of the Yarmouth train, This simply meant that those facing the engine were now sitting back to the engine.

"Well, if that ent a rum'un," said Billy. "I hev bin a'sittin' oppersit yew - an'now yew're a' sittin' oppersit ter me."

Peace Work

Old George's wife had died and he called in the undertaker who asked when the funeral would take place.

"I should like ter bury the poor ole gal termorrer week." said George.

"Tomorrow week?" exclaimed the undertaker. "That means a lapse of eight days. Any special reason for that?"

"Well, thass like this here, Marster" said George. "We'd bin married fer 64 year, and we allus reckoned when we wuz courtin' that if we wuz ever ter git married we'd hev a quiet week on our own.

"This is the only charnse I're had - and, blarst, I'm gorn ter tearke it!"

Return Trip

Old John saved up to buy a bike. He told his pals on the farm that he would be able to go to Swaffham to see his sister on Sundays.

One Monday morning they asked how he had got on biking to Swaffham.

"Well, by the time I git ter Dereham, I wuz wholly wore out, so I tanned rownd and hossed hoom agin'."

"Blarst, thass only harf way", they said.

"I know" said John,. "I'll hatter dew th'uther harf next week."

Ideal Bait

"How many fish have you caught?" asked the stranger as old George sat patiently on the bank.

"Well, " said the old boy thoughtfully, "If I land this one I'm arter, an' then tew more - I'll hev three!"

Patient Lament

Norfolk people have been known to make molehills out of mountains.

A village doctor was motoring round a corner when he collided with one of his patients, a big, hefty man on a bicycle. The doctor hastily got out of his car to help the unfortunate cyclist, who had been sent flying into a ditch full of nettles, brambles and muddy water.

"Are you all right, Herbert?" he asked anxiously.

Herbert rose slowly to his feet, brushed himself down and stretched carefully.

"Yis thankyer, doctor ... 'sept fer a bit of a cowld."

Prize Remarks

Harry won a goat in a raffle at the local fete. A few weeks later his mate Charlie called to ask how the goat was getting on.

"He's gittin' on orryte" said Harry, rather mysteriously.

"Where hev yew put 'im?" asked Charlie.

"In the bedroom alonger my missus."

"Cor blarst me!" exclaimed Charlie. "What 'bowt the smell?"

"Tell yer the trewth" said Harry, "th'ole goot dunt fare ter mind that a mite!"

Tell yer the trewth . . . th'ole goot dunt fare ter mind that a mite!

Back to Basics

A city gent was looking round an old country cottage with a view to buying it. The tenant was a stout old man.

Noting how small the privy was at the top of the garden, the prospective buyer suggested he must find it hard to turn round in such a tiny space.

"Blarst me" exclaimed the old man, "I dunt tarn round in there. I undew my brearces outside - then I back in!"

Playing by Ear

A farmer in the village was a good sort and would help anyone. Unfortunately, he was almost stone deaf.

Living nearby was a cattle drover who was usually hard up and on the cadge. One day he met the farmer and shouted at him: "Lend me sixpence, ole partner!"

The farmer put his hand to his other ear and said: "What dew yew say?" Going round the other side, the drover shouted: "Lend me harf a crown, ole partner!"

The farmer shook his head.

"Yew're got the wrong lug. Go yew round tew the tanner side!"

Timely Advice

A young man bought an old grandfather clock at an auction in the market town. Putting it on his shoulder he set off for home.

But going round a corner he bumped into an old lady and knocked her into the gutter. He apologised profusely.

She looked up and exclaimed: "Why the davil dunt yew look where yew're a'goin' tew, yew sorft young fewl. An' why dunt yew wear a wristwatch like eny other sensible passun!"

A Good Line

The man on the bridge addressed the solitary fisherman. "Any luck?" he asked.

"Any luck? Why, I pulled sixty pike outer here yisterday" replied the fisherman.

"Do you know who I am?" said the man.

"No" said the fisherman.

"Well, I am the chief magistrate for this area and all this estate is mine."

"An' dew yew know who I am?" asked the fisherman.

"No"

"Well, I'm the biggest liar in East Anglia!"

Chapter Four

Round the Village

Enjoy yourself now. These are the good old days you're going to miss later.

The word "village" remains touched with a romance not even the most bloated examples of over-development can totally destroy.

It still stands for roots and durability in uncertain times, a place from which strength and reassurance can be drawn, a haven of togetherness for natives and newcomers who refuse to be carried out on the commuter-and-dormitory tide.

The rural resistance movement knows the true value of a sense of humour, stories told at each other's expense dominating the programme.

"You'll never guess what that new woman at Lilac Cottage put in her tea at the whist drive ... Did you see that bit in the parish magazine about Walter's marrows? ... Talk about a colour clash, but what else can you expect from someone born in Suffolk!"

We know now why our smaller communities are so anxious to keep a full set of facilities - school, shop, pub, church, chapel, village hall, bus service and a lively parish council. They are all vital links in the mardling chain. Locals don't like to repeat gossip - but what else are they supposed to do with it?

Of course, a yarn told in the shop on a Monday morning has gained considerable weight by the time it is presented in the pub on Friday night. Embroidery (let's not call it blatant exaggeration) is a village craft open to all, and newcomers soon learn the value of enrolling for a few handy classes.

Familiarity removes much of the sting from village humour, although the few who won't, or can't play ball have to put up with extra rations. "Can't take a joke" usually means there are sterner tests on the way!

Party Time

It was election time and the canvasser was busy knocking on village doors. At one house a young lady appeared in curlers with about three inches of ash dangling from her cigarette.

"I wonder if you would be so kind as to tell me for whom you are likely to vote in the forthcoming election." said the canvasser.

The young woman looked at him for some time, cleared her throat and replied very slowly:

"Thass like this here ole partner. I hev bin in Learber three times fer bein' ser Librul. So I reckon I'm gorn fer that Contraceptive lot this time."

I reckun I'm gorn fer that Contraceptive lot this time.

Colour Scheme

Morning service had just finished at the village church when the verger stood up to make an announcement.

"Will them what hev them there hassocks and prayer books an' the like, please tearke 'em hoom, cors termorrer we're a'gorn ter start whitewashin' the walls pink!"

A Nice Change

It was a pleasant summer evening and the rector was taking a stroll through the village. Meeting Bertie, one of his parishioners, he bade him "Good evening" and added: "I presume you too are out enjoying this wonderful fresh air?"

"Why yis, Wikker, that I am. Yew want a bit o' fresh air arter bein' cooped up in a forty acre fild all day!"

If at First . . .

Amos was surprised to see the boy Jack walking along the village street in his working clothes.

"I thowt yew wuz a'gettin' wed terday."

"Yis, bor" said Jack. "So I should he' bin, but I couldn't rightly mearke up m'mind. So I tossed up forrit. Hids I dew - tearles I dunt.

"Blarst me if I dint hatter toss up dozen times afore that cum down tearles!"

On the Move

Old Bob had just come back from a ride in his nephew's new sports car. He called at the village pub for his usual pint.

"Well, bor, what did yer think onnit?" asked the landlord. "Did yew go farst?"

"Farst, bor? I'll say we went farst. A'cummin back we wholly went!"

Opportunity Knocks

A drunk walked into church and the confessional by mistake. The priest heard him come in and sat on the other side for five minutes.

Eventually, he knocked on the wall. The drunk awoke, rather startled, and whispered very loudly:

"Thash no good knockin', ole partner - ent no pearper this side nyther."

Thash no good knockin', ole partner - ent no pearper this side nyther!

Time Flies

It was a bit of a puzzle to regulars at The Eradicated Coypu. For several nights Ezra had been in - and he stopped to play cards and dominoes and to sink a few pints.

It was most unlike his wife to allow him such luxuries. Bill thought he'd ask how she was.

"Oh, " said Ezra, "she's in horspital."

"Sorry ter hear that, ole bewty. How long hev she bin there?"

"Well, bor" said Ezra, "in three weeks she'll he'bin there nearly a munth."

Shelling Out

Ezra called at the village shop to buy a dozen eggs. As the shopkeeper began to serve him, Ezra said: " Now hold yew hard! I want the wuns what the yeller-legged hins lay."

With a puzzled look the shopkeeper told Ezra if he had any way of telling which ones they were, he could pick them out himself.

Ezra did just that - he picked out the biggest dozen he could find.

A Good Drop

Ike was out in his pony and trap when he came across a village pub he had never seen before. The barmaid was standing at the door.

"Nut tew bizzy, then?" said Ike. "What's yer ale like?"

"Thass fine ale, Marster" she replied.

"Well, I'd better try a pint an' see what I reckun." said Ike.

The barmaid went in and returned with a pint tankard. Ike soon downed it.

"Better mearke sure" said Ike. "Let's hev nuther wun." He soon consumed that and called for a third. Then he got out of the trap and tied his pony to a post.

"I reckun yew're right, gal. Thass a nice drop o'ale. Think I'll cum in an' hev sum!"

43

Wise Choice

A little old lady was shopping at the local greengrocers. She asked for three pounds of potatoes.

"Dew yew want the large 'uns or the small 'uns?"

"Oh, I'll tearke the little 'uns ... I find them big 'uns tew heavy ter carry."

Happy Release

Hector took two dozen empty beer bottles back to The Eradicated Coypu. He placed his full bag on the counter.

"Dead 'uns?" inquired the landlord.

"Yis," said Hector, "an' I wuz with 'em when they wuz a'dyin'."

A Lead Story

Obadiah lived in a caravan. One day, the local policeman saw a dog tied to the caravan and asked Obadiah if he had got a licence.

"No, that I hent - an' I hent got the munny ter buy wun nyther."

The policeman told him he'd have to get one. Later that day Obadiah turned up at the policeman's house and produced a licence.

"You told me this morning you had no money. So where have you got it from all of a sudden?"

"I sold the dawg."

Fishy Tale

Once a week Joe visited the little village with his donkey and cart selling fish. On this occasion a woman popped her head out of the upstairs window and shouted: "Dunt want nun o'yar fish this week. What I hed larst week'd gorn orff."

"Well, thass yor bloomin' fault" Joe yelled back. "If yew'd bort it the week afore, that would he'bin orryte!"

Matching Pair

Mabel decided to change her rather ancient Morris Minor and took a fancy to a little orange Fiat from the village garage.

She wanted to show off her new motor to her friend Ada, and so invited her for a ride into town to do a bit of shopping. Halfway there, the car stopped. Mabel couldn't get it to start again.

They both got out and opened up the front bonnet to see if they could spot what was wrong.

"Oh Mabel!" said Ada. "Reckun yew've lorst the engine."

"Never mind" said Mabel, "there's nuther wun in the back!"

Chapter Five

Hello

Stranger . . .

Never miss an opportunity to make others happy,
even if you have to leave them alone to do it

If country folk are good at taking the rise out of each other, these antics can pale into nothing alongside treatment reserved for less-than-gracious "furriners".

Devastation comes to the fore, and we like to think it has been going on ever since the first invaders dropped anchor, waded ashore and assumed those funny little peasants were there for the taking.

Some of our best rural yarns spotlight this delightful knack of turning the tables on a prissy or pretentious inquisitor out to score cheap points. There may be a class element involved as the well-heeled executive opens his car window at the touch of a button to summon a village ancient balanced precariously on a rusty bicycle making its slow progress uphill against an icy wind. But it has more to do with objections to manner and assumption than making instant comparisons about material possessions.

"I say, Jimmy old chap, could you tell me the way to Swaffham?"

"How did you know my name wuz Jimmy?"

"Oh, I just guessed it, old boy."

"Rite, ole partner, well you kin jist guess the ruddy way ter Swaffham!"

Country people naturally resent the implication that they are there for the convenience of swish travellers with a tendency to patronise, rebuke or stamp their feet when instant enlightenment is not forthcoming:

"Well, I must say you seem pretty stupid to me."

"I mite be stupid, ole bewty, but I ent lorst!"

NELSON TOUCH

A smart chap from a national television documentary department was asking about Lord Nelson's connections with a certain Norfolk village. He wasn't making much progress.

He saw old Billy sipping his half of mild in the corner of the pub and said rather sarcastically:

"Now, pop, what can you tell me about Nelson? You do remember Nelson, don't you?"

"Yis," said old Billy, "but I'll tell yer suffin' ... I still liked his farther best."

Telling Pace

John was busy trimming his hedge when a stranger came up and asked how long it would take to walk into the village.

"Carnt rightly say" said John. The stranger walked off in a huff. Then John called him back.

"Reckun that'll teake yew 'bowt five minnits."

"Why on earth couldn't you tell me that in the first place?"

"Well, bor, I dint know how farst yew wuz a'gorn ter walk then!"

Quick Work

George was showing an American tourist around the village.

"Thass our chatch ... took nigh on twetty year ter build centuries ago."

"Waal," said the American, "guess in Texas we could erect one in five."

George then pointed out the new council school.

"What 'bowt that, then? Took only nine munth ter build."

"Waal," said the American, "guess back home we can erect a school in six months."

They turned a corner and there stood the village hall.

"Say, buddy, what's that building then?"

"Dunno" said George. "That wunt there when I cum ter work this mornin'."

Subtle Hint

The ancient verger acted as guide for a tour of the village church, and gave a most detailed history of the building.

When he had finished he invited the visitors to place a donation on the collection plate near the door. They all did so - except for one well-heeled gentleman in a tweed suit.

As the party boarded their bus, the verger called to the man who had failed to make a contribution:

"'Scuse me, ole partner, but if yew should find yew hent got your wallet when yew git hoom, jist yew remember yew dint tearke it out here."

Wrong Brand

In the early days of the motor car, a smart model conked out in a country village. A crowd of locals soon gathered round.

The driver, wearing goggles and all the latest gear, tinkered with the engine for about half an hour and then turned to one of the watching lads.

"I say old chap, just nip down the King's Head and get me some pliers."

The lad returned a few minutes later.

"Werry sorry, guv, I coont git no pliers ... so I bought twetty Gold Flearke."

Very Helpful

Stanley got up to answer a knock on the door. There stood a stranger.

"Does Fred Cummings live here?"

"No, he dunt."

"Well, would you happen to know if he lives in this street?"

"Yis, he dew live in this street."

"Would you happen to know at which number?"

"No, - but that'll be on the door."

Just Too Late

"What a pretty little village!" enthused the woman tourist to her husband. "Let's go and ask that dear old chap over there all about it."

The village sage was sitting outside the pub minding his own business.

"Would you happen to be the oldest inhabitant of this enchanting hamlet?" asked the woman.

"Blarst, no" he replied, "he went an'died larst week."

On Right Track

A couple of American servicemen were waiting for a train, and they kept on telling the old porter they had bigger and faster trains back home. They were just about to elaborate when a fast train to Ipswich raced through, hauled by a Britannia class locomotive.

"Gee, buddy, what was that?" asked one of the Americans.

"Oh," said the porter, "That wuz old Tom dewin'a bit o' shuntin'."

Oh, that wuz old Tom dewin'a bit o' shuntin'!

Winding Up

A stranger pulled up to chat with a local veteran who was lighting his pipe by the gate to the field.

"You've got some rare winding roads around here." he suggested.

"Ah, bor, that we hev. They dew reckun as how them what laid 'em out liked to keep the wind at their backs. So every time that c h a n g e d direckshun, so did the road!"

. . . they liked to keep the wind at their backs!

Chapter Six

The Last Word . . .

Don't finish anything you aren't able to start

One of the most endearing traits of country people is an uncanny ability to turn apparent defeat into possible victory, to bounce off the ropes with a stunning verbal blow. Endearing? Well, it is if you are not on the receiving end.

Lady of house: *"You have enough brass in your neck to make a copper kettle."*

Domestic servant: *"Yis, an' there's enough water in yar ole skull ter fill it!"*

No room left for a comeback or a compromise, although the dangers of employing such juicy repartee are obvious. Would that lady of the house have smiled in appreciation at such ready wit or settled instead for instant dismissal? Perhaps the cheeky domestic had arrived in the first place because of her outspoken nature and this was the next trap set for her.

Easy to chuckle from the sidelines, and we all like to see balloons of pomposity pricked, but determination to go for the last word can be high-risk business. On occasions there's blatant egging-on from those much too scared to make a stand themselves. "Go on, you show 'em who's boss!"

Of course, there's some protection in pretending to be an innocent abroad - and the genuine rustic simpleton stars in many good stories - but ignorance is no excuse in a cosmopolitan world!"

The Whole Truth

Horry found his pretty young bride crying her eyes out when he came home.

"I feel suffin' awful" she said. "When I wuz pressin'yar new suit I barnt a gret big hole in the seat o' yar trowsers."

"Dunt yew worry so" said Horry. "Yew muster fergot I hev that extra pair o'trowsers ter go wi' that suit."

"I remembered orryte" said his wife. "I cut a piece outer them ter patch the hole!"

55

Some Welcome!

A Suffolk chap was returning to his home village after making his fortune abroad. He had been away for ten years.

As he got off the train at the little station he looked round for old friends he was sure would be there to meet him. The platform was deserted.

Rather crestfallen, he called for the porter to carry his bags. As the porter emerged, the homecoming fellow eagerly recognised an old school friend. But before he could say anything, the porter spoke ...

"Oh, hello Fred - what are yew gorn away?"

Sign Language

An elderly lady of sound means was interviewing a young Norfolk girl with a view to engaging her as a domestic servant.

"Well, Audrey, I think you will suit me very well, provided you always remember I am a lady of very few words. So, if I beckon you with my finger like this ... you will know that I mean come here."

"Thass orryte, ma'm" said Audrey cheerfully. "And if I shearke my skull like this, yew'll know I arnt a' cummin'!"

Tuning In

Bob was a bit hard of hearing, but simply couldn't afford to buy himself a hearing aid. He draped a bit of picture cord over his ear instead.

"Wass the good o'that?" said old friend Bill. "Dunt mearke yew hear enny better."

"No, bor, praps that dunt" replied Bob, "but now when folks speak ter me they holler."

City Lights

A village lad was making his first visit after dark to the big city of Norwich. He was entranced by the sight of the castle in all its floodlit glory.

As he stood admiring, a lady of the night edged towards him in her high heels and fur coat. She didn't get any reaction, so she clicked her heels on the pavement. Still no response. So she tugged his overalls and whispered seductively: "Dew yew want a bit?"

His eyes still aloft, he replied: "Blarst me! What are they gorter knock it down?"

Blarst me! What are they gorter knock it down?!

Current Rate

A girl swimming off the Suffolk coast was having trouble getting ashore owing to the undercurrent. She called to a boatman to come to her assistance.

He took no notice but she eventually reached the shore unaided.

She asked the boatman sharply why he had not heeded her call.

He replied "The larst gal I helped, she only gi'me harf a crown. We git five bob fer a body."

Capital Reply

A country girl went up to London into service at a big house.

There were many other servants there who constantly ribbed her about being a country cousin.

One day after a shopping expedition she returned and rang the doorbell for admittance. The footman who let her in remarked: "Well, if it isn't our little country cousin back again!"

She looked him up and down and then said, very deliberately: "There, now, ent Lunnun a wholly wunnerful plearce ... all yew're gotter dew is push a button and out pop a fewl!"

Tough Choice

Ezra's wife was at home alone when the insurance man called in the hope of attracting a new customer.

"Oh, I leave them sort o'things ter my ole man." she said.

"So you don't know what you would get if your husband died?" asked the agent.

"Well, no, not zakkly." said Ezra's wife. "But I think I'd git a budgie or a poodle!"

Handsome Crop

They say country folk tend to exaggerate. Well, one Norfolk farmer told a worker to go and borrow a cross-cut saw ... his mangolds were so big he couldn't get them on to the cart. Off went the worker.

"Please Sar, my Marster would like ter borrer yar crorscut. His mangles are ser big he carnt lift 'em itter the cart."

"Well, bor" replied the neighbouring farmer, "jist yew tell yar marster I'm wholly sorry but my crorscut is stuck in a tearter!"

Not Her Fault

A boarding house landlady at Lowestoft advertised for an extra maid during the holiday season. The girl who took the job was dismissed at the end of her first week.

When she asked the reason why, the landlady produced two plates betraying evidence of unsatisfactory washing-up.

"Just look at these, Emily." she scowled. "What have you to say for yourself?"

"Well, ma'am" came the reply. "I'm happy ter arnser fer them black thumbmarks - but that there dried mustard wuz on afore I cum!"

Slow Payers

The farmer's maid refused to get up one morning. The farmer, thinking she was ill, called the doctor.

"Now, what's the matter, Mary?"

"Ent noffin the matter."

"Well, why don't you get up then?

"I ent gorn tew. They owe me tew munth wearges, an' I dunt git up til they pay up."

The doctor smiled. "Oh that's it - well, shift over. They've owed me a bill for two years!"

Fit for the Job

"Yis, ma'am" said Amy, the prospective maid, "I hev seven excellent refrunces."

"That sounds very good, I must say. How long have you been in service?"

"Well, ma'am I hev bin in service since I left school larst munth."

Food for Thought

An old countryman was very ill in bed and hadn't been allowed anything to eat for several days.

Then the doctor called and after a lengthy examination he told the wife her husband wouldn't last much longer, and so he could have anything he liked to eat.

After the doctor had gone the woman called up the stairs: "Fred, doctor say yew kin hev ennything yew like ter eat."

The old man called back with something approaching delight: "Cor blarst me. I'd wholly like some o' that there ham yew're bin a'cookin' down there. That smell bewtiful."

To which came the sharp retort: "Yew carn't he' that. Thass fer yer fewnrul."

Chapter Seven

Pew and Pulpit

> *"Come to morning service early if you want a good back seat!"*

Church and chapel remain at the core of country life in many places - even if some people use them only for christenings, weddings and funerals.

Parsons and lay preachers have inspired countless good stories over the years, but a small, select collection can underline the significance of their roles on the local scene and the genuine affection in which most of them have been held.

Memories of rough-hewn but passionate Methodist brethren and eccentric but well-loved village clergymen do the regular rounds. I recall an old country preacher who came on his bike with a Bible and hymn book in his saddlebag. He had a habit of reminding us all that we were miserable sinners. If we wanted forgiveness the creed was "git on yar knees ternite and put it rite!"

Another chapel regular used to say by way of introduction: "I compare yew lot tew the contents of a gret ole Christmas puddin' - an' I am the long-handled spoon woss bin sent ter stir yew up!"

Preachers often had double appointments, afternoon and evening at the same chapel, and so received regular invitations out to tea. I remember one dear lady entertaining the preacher to tea, and before the evening service he said: "I would like to thank Miss Brown for her hospitality."

She shouted out: "That wunt horspitality, bruther - that wuz stewed rubub!"

Rare Recipe

A good Norfolk man died and went to Heaven. St Peter met him at the Pearly Gates and asked where he came from.

"Cromer".

St Peter shook his head.

"Rum ole dew, bor ... carnt see 'em mearkin' Norfolk dumplins fer one!"

Early Shower

A country rector was visited by a lady parishioner rather early in the morning. She was very agitated. "Sorry ter trubble yer this tyme o' the mornin', Rector, but I thowt yew cood intarpret a dream I hed larst night. I dremt I saw my Willum - yew 'member him, dunt yer? Well, he cum an' stand by m' bedside, an' oh, he did look bewtiful! He hev a crown on his skull an' a harp in his hand an' he's a' wearin' a long white robe. Oh he did look ser bewtiful!"

The old lady looked pleadingly at the rector: "Dew yew think that mean rain?"

All of a Flutter

Three country vicars were having trouble with bats in their churches. They met over coffee to discuss what progress was being made.

"I put all mine in a cardboard box and took them miles away." said the first. "Unfortunately, they beat me back to the church."

"I rang the bells non-stop for five hours" said the second. "But the only result of that was to make me deaf."

"I hev got rid o' mine" said the third. His colleagues were bursting to know the secret.

"Well, all I dun was ter baptise 'em an' confarm 'em. I hent seen 'em since!"

Wise Guy?

The vicar noticed how old Ezra always bent the knee when both Christ and the Devil were mentioned.

Asked about this apparently contradictory behaviour, he replied: "Well, bor, that corst noffin ter be perlite ... and yew never know!"

Fine Tribute

Shortly after his arrival in a new country parish, the vicar was asked to conduct a funeral service.

He announced: "I am very sorry that I cannot pay tribute to the deceased as I did not know him. But if any of you would like to say a few words, please feel free to do so."

There was complete silence in the little village church. The vicar tried again.

"Now please do not be shy, I'm sure someone would like to say a kindly word about our dear departed friend."

Another long silence. Suddenly, a voice from the back muttered:

"His bruther wuz wass!"

Close Secret

The new village parson asked old George the best way to keep his flock interested.

"Well, ole partner, we allus reckon the secret of a good sarmun is a good berginnin' and a good endin'" said George.

The parson smiled his thanks. But George hadn't quite finished ....

"And leavin' 'em as close tergether as possible!"

Good Timing

A bishop went to stay overnight with one of his country clergymen.

Coming down to breakfast, the bishop was surprised to hear "Rock of Ages" rising lustily forth from the kitchen.

Pleased to imagine that this was an early morning form of worship, he asked the parson's son to tell him who was singing.

"That's dear old Mabel, the cook" replied the boy. "She always sings "Rock of Ages" as she boils eggs for breakfast.

"Three verses for soft-boiled and five verses for hard boiled."

Time Drags

At an especially long church service one Sunday morning most of the congregation were on the verge of nodding off.

The sermon seemed to be going on for hours. Suddenly, a plaintive voice came from the back of the church:

"Martha, is it still Sunday?"

Standing Vote

Old Jimmy was inclined to fall asleep in church, and so the vicar thought he would teach him a little lesson.

That Sunday morning in the middle of his sermon he could see Jimmy had nodded off, so he said in a very soft voice: "Everybody who wants to go to Hell ...." and then he shouted at the top of his voice ... "STAND UP!"

Old Jimmy woke with a start, jumped up and looked round. He could see no other members of the congregation on their feet. He looked towards the pulpit and said:

"Dunno what we're a'votin' for, Wikker, but that look like yew an' me are the only ones for it!"

Sound Advice

Notice in a Parish Church Newsletter:
"Tonight's sermon: 'What is Hell?'. Come early and listen to our choir practice."

What is Hell? . . . Come and listen to our choir practice!

Cuttings from Parish Church Newsletters

ALLS WELL …
"Michael Jones and Jessie Carter were married in this church recently. So ends a friendship which began in schooldays."

GRAND FINALE
"The service today will end with 'Little Drops of Water'. One of the men will start quietly and the rest of the congregation will join in."

DAMP DOUBLE
"This afternoon there will be a meeting in the south and north ends of this church. Children will be baptised at both ends."

BASEMENT BARGAIN
"The ladies of the church have cast off clothing of every kind, and they can be seen in the church basement on Friday afternoon."

A MAT FINISH?
"On Sunday, a special collection will be taken to defray the expense of the new carpet. All wishing to do something on the carpet, please come forward and get a piece of paper."

PARSON PHASE
"The Ladies Literary Society will meet on Wednesday. Mrs Johnson will sing 'Put Me In My Little Bed', accompanied by the parson."

FOND GOODBYE
"The Rector will present his farewell sermon, after which the choir will sing; 'Break forth into joy'."

SEASONAL GIFT
"This being Easter Sunday, we will ask Mrs Brown to come and lay an egg on the altar."

Chapter Eight

Just a Few More . . .

Laughter improves your face value

As emphasised at the outset, the majority of country yarns with a distinctive local flavour were meant to be told to an attentive audience rather than be collated and read in a volume like this. Indeed, some favourites could well be appearing in print for the first time, and yet they will carry a familiar ring among those who appreciate true culture.

Most amusing stories stand regular repetition, although personalities and locations may be changed in keeping with a more mobile age than the one in which they were first crafted and shared. I have heard several versions of the same yarn - and laughed heartily at all of them. Good material is both durable and adaptable.

Of course, there's a heavy tang of nostalgia hanging over many of these stories. The further away we find ourselves from the stage of their rustic fashioning, the stronger becomes our affection for a "golden era" of country life and humour.

That's the nature of the feast. Snapshots of characters and scenes with an endearing quality that defies passing fashion and changing patterns.

Country writer Clarence Henry Warren said over half a century ago: "It is one of the most attractive features of country humour that it never quite loses its freshness. It may be passed on from generation to generation, but it remains a coin whose mintage is never dulled with use."

Go on, give that coin a few more flips - and get ready to entertain if anyone should call "tales"!

Family Ties

A Suffolk chap lived at home with his parents in the country. He was a quiet sort, so it came as a bit of a surprise when he arrived back at the house with a young lady on his arm one Sunday.

"Mum! Dad!" he called. "Cum an' meet Lucy! We're walkin' out tergether, an if things go orryte, we'll be gittin' married."

His father took him to one side. "Cum here, boy" he said, and led him into the scullery.

"Yew carnt marry har."

"Why nut?"

"Cors she's yar sister."

The boy was most upset and didn't want any tea. In fact, he moped all round the house for several weeks.

A few months later, just as Mother was again preparing the Sunday spread, the boy arrived home with another girl on his arm. He beamed proudly.

"Mum! Dad! This here is Mabel. She's my new galfriend. We're walkin' out tergether and if everything go orryte, we're gorter git married."

"Cum here, boy" said Father and wheeled him in to the scullery.

"Yew carnt marry har."

"But whyever nut?"

"Cors she's yar sister!"

This time the boy was beyond consolation. He sat on his own in the front room without a word to his parents for over a week. Eventually his mother brought him a cup of tea and asked what was the matter.

"I'm right fed up" he said.

"What are yer fed up abowt?"

"Every time I bring a nice gal hoom and say I'm gorter marry har, Father tearke me inter the scullery an' say 'Yew carnt marry har', an'I say 'Why nut?', an' he say 'Cors thass yar sister!'. That git on my wick!"

His mother gave him a long, lingering look and then said: "Oh ... yew dunt watter tearke no notice o' him. He ent no relearshun o' yars."

Doctor's Orders

Ephraim's wife hadn't been feeling very well and so she went to see her doctor. On her return Ephraim asked how she had got on.

"Well, he say what I need is a long holiday by the sea. Where dew yew think I orter go?"

Ephraim replied quickly: "Ter see anuther docter, I shud reckun!"

Using His Head

Amos was up before the local magistrates. He had hit the road foreman on the head with his shovel after an argument as to how a stretch of village road should be repaired to prevent a recurring puddle every time it rained.

The Chairman asked Amos why he had hit the foreman on the head.

"Well, yar honner, we wunt a'gittin' nowhere, so I thowt thass where the trubble lie!"

Noises Off

Jem was celebrating his 100th birthday. He told the local newspaper he owed his longevity to never having touched a drop of alcohol.

A few days later a young lady called from a Temperance magazine and said she wanted to interview him.

Jem agreed and confirmed that he had never touched alcohol. "Thass why I hev reached three figgers, my bewty."

The young lady was about to leave when there came an almighty banging from the room above.

"What on earth is that?" she asked.

"Oh, that'll be Dad - drunk as a lord agin!"

Norfolk Air

Jacob had to move from his beloved countryside in his later years to live with his daughter in London. He couldn't acclimatise to life in the big city. He fell ill and it soon became clear he had reached his final innings. The family gathered round the bed.

"What can we do for you?" they asked.

"Only thing what'll dew me enny good now is a drop o' Norfolk air" murmured the old man.

"Don't you fret" said son-in-law Fred. "I'll see to that."

Next day, Fred got his bike out and set off for Norfolk. He reached Norwich Cattle Market on the Saturday morning. There he let the wind out of his tyres, pumped them up again and headed back for London.

Opening his front door he took the bike inside and carried it up the stairs.

"Here comes the boy Fred" they cried. "You'll soon be all right now, Jacob."

Fred bent down, unscrewed the valve and let all the wind out of the tyre. Old Jacob took one whiff - and passed away.

"Oh, dear" exclaimed his daughter. "I don't understand that. I thought it would do him good."

"Yes" said Fred, "It's a great pity I got that puncture at Colchester."

Root Cause

Old Barney was getting on in years, but still managed to dig and plant his large cottage garden.

Fred the postman had some letters to deliver at Barney's cottage just as the old boy was about to plant his seed potatoes. Fred thought they didn't look up to much. Nor did Barney, who muttered: "I'll give yew so long. Dew yew dunt cum up, up yew'll cum!"

Honest Lad

Talk in the village pub centred on how they had met their wives. Some said it was at a dance in the village hall. Others recalled how they had been introduced by a friend.

"What abowt yew?" old Tom was asked.

"Well, that so happen I met my missus b' accerdent. So I carnt blearme ennywun!"

Homely Sort

Tom: "How is yar missus?"

Horry: "She hev got culinary thrombosis"

Tom: "Whass that?"

Horry: "She's clot in the kitchen!"

Beyond the Pail

A lad from the country, where the lavatory was at the top of the garden, joined the Army. He was stationed at very modern barracks. His first letter home read like this:

"Dear Dad, This is the life. All mod. cons. Flush toylets etc. When I cum hoom on leave I'll dew away wi' our ole petty at the top of the garden and we'll hev a modern one."

He duly arrived home on leave. On entering the garden gate he threw a hand grenade on to the small building which went up in a cloud of dust. At the same time his father opened the door and said: "Yew shunt he' dun that, boy ... Yar muther wuz in there."

When the old girl emerged from the rubble, covered in dust, straw and odd pieces of brick, the boy said, most contritely, "I'm wholly sorry, Mum."

She replied quietly: "That wunt yar fault, my boy ... that must he' bin suffin I ett"

Careful Does It

Farmer Jim was renowned for taking care of the pennies. So it was with some surprise that his friends discovered he had bought a horse and intended to take up riding.

He went to the local saddler's shop and asked for a spur.

"Dunt yew mean a pair o' spurs?" said the assistant.

"No, I dunt" said Farmer Jim. "I reckun if I kin git one side o' the hoss ter move, th'uther side'll foller."

Can't Fool Him

George and Bert had been detailed to deliver some bits and pieces by tractor and trailer to another farm by the coast.

After finishing the task they decided to go down to the beach to eat their elevenses.

Bert finished drinking his cold tea and wandered down to the sea to fill the bottle with water.

"What ever are yew a'dewin' that for?" asked George.

"Well, the missus hent sin the sea fer ages, so I thowt I'd tearke her sum o'innit hoom."

"Yew sorft ole fewl!" exclaimed George. "That'll bust yar bottle soon's the tide cum in!"

Only Fair

"How's that new baby getting on?" the vicar called as he passed the field where Herbert was working.

"Mornin' wikker. My missus an' yar bearby are dewin' fine."

"My baby? What on earth can you mean?" spluttered the vicar.

"Well, ole partner" said Herbert. "Thass like this here. They allus used ter say the tenth part belong ter the clergy. Thass our tenth child - so I reckun thass yours!"

Sharing Touch

Basil and Martha met at the old people's club. Both widowed, they fell in love and decided to marry.

"What about a wedding list?" asked Basil's daughter.

"There's only wun thing we want, ent there, gal?" he smiled at his intended.

"And what might that be?" asked his daughter.

"My ole cup wunt hold tew sets o'dentchers. We want a gret ole mug fer that!"

Public Warning

Billy walked into the pub carrying a chequered flag.

"Now then," said the landlord. "Hope yew ent gorter start ennything in here!"

Holding Fire!

Much against her wishes, old Mary had a bathroom installed. The vicar called a few weeks later.

"I dare say you find the new bathroom quite convenient" he suggested.

"Well, sar" said Mary, "I hent had occashun ter use it yit!"

Dad Knows Best

A village schoolmaster taking a class in history asked: "Who signed Magna Carta?"

Little Bertie replied: "If yer please, sar, I dint!"

Next day the schoolmaster met Bertie's father. "Your little lad amused me in the class yesterday when I asked who signed Magna Carta and he said 'Please sir, I didn't'."

The dad smiled and replied: "Little beggar ... I bet he did!"

Dry Response

In the early days of the Second World War, two farm labourers were pulling sugar beet on a large open field in driving wind and pouring rain.

One of them had happened to see a newspaper before coming to work. He said to his partner: "I see in the EDP them ole Jarmans hev gone inter Warsaw."

The other tugged at his coat collar, gazed up at the brooding skies and remarked: "Well, they hent got much o' a day fer it, hev they?"

They got on with the job without another word.

Truth In One

Walter was very much overweight. His doctor advised him to take up some form of exercise.

"Go golfing" he told him.

"Thass no good" said Walter. "I hev tried that orridy. If I put the ball where I kin see it, I carnt hit it. If I put it where I kin hit it, I carnt see it!"

Talking Point

Two ancient countrymen met daily to sit outside the village pub, quite content to enjoy the silence for long periods.

One day, Sam spoke: "How' your missus gittin' on, Charlie?"

"Well" came the reply, "I dunt rightly know whass the matter wi' her. She keep on a-jawin an' a-jawin."

Prolonged silence. The suddenly: "Thass a rum'un bowt yar missus, Charlie. What dew she keep a-jawin bowt?"

"I dunno. She dunt say."

Money Talks

The old farmer was dying, and his wife and a few neighbours were sitting by the bed. After a long silence the old man whispered: "I owe Farmer Brown five quid."

His wife commented: "There he go - ramblin' agin."

After another long silence, the old boy started to whisper again: "Farmer Harvey owe me ten quid."

At this his wife said triumphantly: "There he go agin - sensible ter the larst!"

Poor Return

A man was telling his neighbour about the sow he used to keep.

"I hed ter git rid o' her" he said. "She wunt no good."

"How dew yew mean?" asked the neighbour.

"Well, first time she pigged she dint hev enny, an' next time she hed only tew - an' they et each other."

Dinner Time

A parson biking round the village delivering church magazines let them fall onto the muddy road. He picked them up, brushed off the mud and put them into a handkerchief to carry, tying the corner into a knot.

As he continued on his way he came across workmen with the road up. One was using very strong language. The parson went up to him.

"My son, do you know Satan?"

"No, I dunt" said the man. Then he shouted to his mate.

"Harry, dew yew know Satan?"

"No, bor. Why?"

"Well, there's a chap here woss brought his dinner."